TRAVEL LISTOGRAPHY

EXPLORING THE WORLD IN LISTS

CREATED BY LISA NOLA

ILLUSTRATIONS BY KELLY ABELN

CHRONICLE BOOKS
SAN FRANCISCO

Text copyright © 2013 by Lisa Nola
Illustrations copyright © 2013 by Chronicle Books LLC.

ISBN 978-1-4521-1557-3

Manufactured in China

Illustrations and hand lettering by Kelly Abeln

Chronicle Books publishes distinctive books and gifts. From
award-winning children's titles, bestselling cookbooks, and eclec-
tic pop culture to acclaimed works of art and design, stationery,
and journals, we craft publishing that's instantly recognizable for
its spirit and creativity. Enjoy our publishing and become part of
our community at www.chroniclebooks.com.

20 19 18 17 16 15 14 13 12 11

Chronicle Books LLC
680 Second Street
San Francisco, CA 94107
www.chroniclebooks.com

DEDICATED TO MY FRIEND RICHARD

"TRAVEL IS FATAL TO PREJUDICE, BIGOTRY, AND NARROW-MINDEDNESS." —MARK TWAIN

TRAVELING IS A TRANSFORMATIVE EXPERIENCE THAT EXPANDS OUR PERSPECTIVE AND ENRICHES THE CONNECTION WE HAVE TO EACH OTHER. **TRAVEL LISTOGRAPHY** IS YOUR BOOK TO RECORD WHERE YOU'VE BEEN AND WHERE YOU HOPE TO GO. EVEN WRITING DOWN THE PLACES YOU'D LIKE TO VISIT CAN SPARK YOUR IMAGINATION AND BE A REMINDER OF HOW TRULY AMAZING OUR PLANET IS.

WISHING YOU MANY HAPPY ADVENTURES THROUGHOUT YOUR LIFE,

LISA NOLA

WWW. LISTOGRAPHY. COM

HONOLULU, HAWAII

CITIES AND STATES IN THE UNITED STATES

I'VE VISITED:

NEW YORK

TEXAS - HOUSTON

SAN ANTONIO

FLORIDA

HOPE TO VISIT:

☐ LOS ANGELES

☐ LAS VEGAS

☐ SAN FRACISCO

☐

☐

☐

☐

☐

☐

☐

☐

☐

☐

☐

☐

☐

☐

☐

SAMANÁ, DOMINICAN REPUBLIC

CITIES AND COUNTRIES IN NORTH AND CENTRAL AMERICA

I'VE VISITED:

HOPE TO VISIT:

BUENOS AIRES, ARGENTINA

CITIES AND COUNTRIES IN SOUTH AMERICA

I'VE VISITED:

HOPE TO VISIT:

- [ ] BRAZIL
- [ ] ARGENTINA
- [ ] URUAGUAY
- [ ] CHILE
- [ ] PERU
- [ ] COLOMBIA
- [ ] ECUADOR
- [ ] PARAGUAY
- [ ]
- [ ]
- [ ]
- [ ]
- [ ]
- [ ]
- [ ]
- [ ]
- [ ]
- [ ]
- [ ]

CASABLANCA, MOROCCO

CITIES AND COUNTRIES IN AFRICA

I'VE VISITED:

_____

_____

_____

_____

_____

_____

_____

_____

_____

_____

_____

_____

_____

_____

_____

_____

_____

_____

HOPE TO VISIT:

- [ ] BOTSWANA
- [ ] CAPE TOWN
- [ ] ZIMBABWE
- [ ] _____
- [ ] _____
- [ ] _____
- [ ] _____
- [ ] _____
- [ ] _____
- [ ] _____
- [ ] _____
- [ ] _____
- [ ] _____
- [ ] _____
- [ ] _____
- [ ] _____
- [ ] _____
- [ ] _____

VARANASI, INDIA

CITIES AND COUNTRIES IN ASIA

I'VE VISITED:

BANGKOK, THAILAND

HUA HIN, THAILAND

CHIANG MAI, THAILAND

PATTAYA, THAILAND

KOH SAMUI, THAILAND

KRABI, THAILAND

SIEM REAP, CAMBODIA

HO CHI MINH CITY, VIETNAM

HOI AN, VIETNAM

HA LONG BAY, VIETNAM

HANOI, VIETNAM

SINGAPORE

KUALA LUMPUR, MALAYSIA

HOPE TO VISIT:

- [ ] LAOS
- [ ] MYANMAR
- [ ] NEPAL
- [ ] HONG KONG
- [ ] CHINA

CASTRILLO DE MURCIA, SPAIN

CITIES AND COUNTRIES IN EUROPE

I'VE VISITED:

AUSTRIA / SLOVENIA
BELGIUM / SLOVAKIA
FRANCE / LITHUANIA
ITALY / LATVIA
SPAIN
PORTUGAL
CROATIA
GERMANY
GREECE
NETHERLANDS
SWITZERLAND
POLAND
DENMARK
CZECH REPUBLIC
HUNGARY
ROMANIA
CYPRUS
BULGARIA
LUXEMBOURG

HOPE TO VISIT:

☐ FINLAND
☐ ICELAND
☐ UKRAINE
☐ ESTONIA
☐ BELARUS
☐
☐
☐
☐
☐
☐
☐
☐
☐
☐
☐
☐
☐
☐

PAPUA NEW GUINEA

CITIES, COUNTRIES, AND LOCATIONS IN AUSTRALIA, OCEANIA, AND ANTARCTICA

I'VE VISITED:

BALI - UBUD
       SEMINYAK

HOPE TO VISIT:

☐ AUSTRALIA
☐ NEW ZEALAND
☐
☐
☐
☐
☐
☐
☐
☐
☐
☐
☐
☐
☐
☐
☐
☐

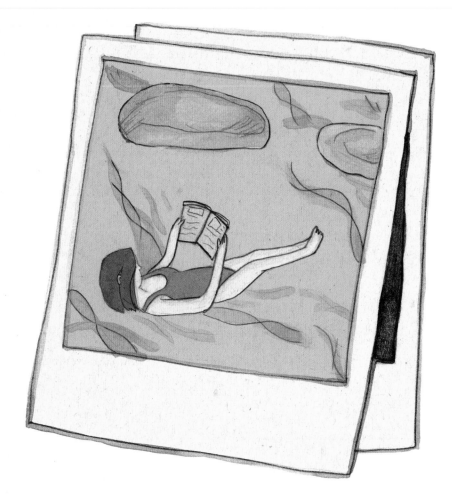

THE DEAD SEA

BEACHES, OCEANS, AND SEAS

I'VE VISITED:

HOPE TO VISIT:

- [ ] ----------------------------
- [ ] ----------------------------
- [ ] ----------------------------
- [ ] ----------------------------
- [ ] ----------------------------
- [ ] ----------------------------
- [ ] ----------------------------
- [ ] ----------------------------
- [ ] ----------------------------
- [ ] ----------------------------
- [ ] ----------------------------
- [ ] ----------------------------
- [ ] ----------------------------
- [ ] ----------------------------
- [ ] ----------------------------
- [ ] ----------------------------
- [ ] ----------------------------
- [ ] ----------------------------
- [ ] ----------------------------
- [ ] ----------------------------

ATLANTIC OCEAN

CAPE COD BAY

NANTUCKET SOUND

N
W E
S

PROVINCETOWN, CAPE COD

COASTAL TOWNS

I'VE VISITED:

HOPE TO VISIT:

ANGKOR WAT, CAMBODIA

MAN—MADE WONDERS

I'VE VISITED:

_____

_____

_____

_____

_____

_____

_____

_____

_____

_____

_____

_____

_____

_____

_____

_____

_____

HOPE TO VISIT:

☐ _____

☐ _____

☐ _____

☐ _____

☐ _____

☐ _____

☐ _____

☐ _____

☐ _____

☐ _____

☐ _____

☐ _____

☐ _____

☐ _____

☐ _____

☐ _____

☐ _____

AURORA BOREALIS

NATURAL WONDERS, FORMATIONS, AND PHENOMENA

I'VE VISITED:

HOPE TO VISIT:

- [ ]
- [ ]
- [ ]
- [ ]
- [ ]
- [ ]
- [ ]
- [ ]
- [ ]
- [ ]
- [ ]
- [ ]
- [ ]
- [ ]
- [ ]
- [ ]
- [ ]
- [ ]
- [ ]

RAPA NUI NATIONAL PARK, EASTER ISLAND

WORLD HERITAGE SITES

I'VE VISITED:

HOPE TO VISIT:

BIG BEN

HISTORIC SITES AND LANDMARKS

I'VE VISITED:

HOPE TO VISIT:

DEVILS TOWER NATIONAL MONUMENT, WYOMING

MONUMENTS AND MEMORIALS

I'VE VISITED:

_____
_____
_____
_____
_____
_____
_____
_____
_____
_____
_____
_____
_____
_____
_____
_____
_____
_____

HOPE TO VISIT:

- [ ] _____
- [ ] _____
- [ ] _____
- [ ] _____
- [ ] _____
- [ ] _____
- [ ] _____
- [ ] _____
- [ ] _____
- [ ] _____
- [ ] _____
- [ ] _____
- [ ] _____
- [ ] _____
- [ ] _____
- [ ] _____
- [ ] _____
- [ ] _____
- [ ] _____

KOREAN

WORLD CUISINES

I'VE TRIED:

SPANISH

THAI

BALINESE

FRENCH

GERMAN

POLISH

HOPE TO TRY:

☐
☐
☐
☐
☐
☐
☐
☐
☐
☐
☐
☐
☐
☐
☐
☐
☐
☐
☐

KINDERKOOKKAFÉ, NETHERLANDS

RESTAURANTS AROUND THE WORLD

I'VE TRIED:

DINE IN THE DARK (KL)

HOPE TO TRY:

THE PANDA

ANIMALS IN THE WILD

I'VE SEEN:

HOPE TO SEE:

NATIONAL ZOOLOGICAL GARDENS OF SOUTH AFRICA

ZOOS, AQUARIUMS, WILDLIFE PARKS, AND REFUGES

I'VE VISITED:

BERLIN

HOPE TO VISIT:

DOG BARK PARK INN, IDAHO

PLACES TO SPEND THE NIGHT

I'VE STAYED:

HOPE TO STAY:

☐
☐
☐
☐
☐
☐
☐
☐
☐
☐
☐
☐
☐
☐
☐
☐
☐
☐
☐

CLIFF JUMP, MEXICO

OUTDOOR ADVENTURES

I'VE EXPERIENCED:

_____

_____

_____

_____

_____

_____

_____

_____

_____

_____

_____

_____

_____

_____

_____

_____

_____

HOPE TO EXPERIENCE:

☐ _____

☐ _____

☐ _____

☐ _____

☐ _____

☐ _____

☐ _____

☐ _____

☐ _____

☐ _____

☐ _____

☐ _____

☐ _____

☐ _____

☐ _____

☐ _____

☐ _____

ROUTE 66

ROAD TRIPS

I'VE DONE:

HOPE TO DO:

- [ ]
- [ ]
- [ ]
- [ ]
- [ ]
- [ ]
- [ ]
- [ ]
- [ ]
- [ ]
- [ ]
- [ ]
- [ ]
- [ ]
- [ ]
- [ ]
- [ ]
- [ ]

HIGHWAY 1, CALIFORNIA

PRETTIEST DRIVES

I'VE DRIVEN:

HOPE TO DRIVE:

☐ ------------------------------
☐ ------------------------------
☐ ------------------------------
☐ ------------------------------
☐ ------------------------------
☐ ------------------------------
☐ ------------------------------
☐ ------------------------------
☐ ------------------------------
☐ ------------------------------
☐ ------------------------------
☐ ------------------------------
☐ ------------------------------
☐ ------------------------------
☐ ------------------------------
☐ ------------------------------
☐ ------------------------------
☐ ------------------------------
☐ ------------------------------

MONUMENT VALLEY, UTAH

CAMPING SPOTS

I'VE CAMPED:

_____
_____
_____
_____
_____
_____
_____
_____
_____
_____
_____
_____
_____
_____
_____
_____
_____
_____
_____

HOPE TO CAMP:

☐ _____
☐ _____
☐ _____
☐ _____
☐ _____
☐ _____
☐ _____
☐ _____
☐ _____
☐ _____
☐ _____
☐ _____
☐ _____
☐ _____
☐ _____
☐ _____
☐ _____
☐ _____
☐ _____

MILFORD SOUND HIKE, NEW ZEALAND

HIKES

I'VE DONE:

HOPE TO DO:

☐ ------------------------

☐ ------------------------

☐ ------------------------

☐ ------------------------

☐ ------------------------

☐ ------------------------

☐ ------------------------

☐ ------------------------

☐ ------------------------

☐ ------------------------

☐ ------------------------

☐ ------------------------

☐ ------------------------

☐ ------------------------

☐ ------------------------

☐ ------------------------

☐ ------------------------

☐ ------------------------

EVERGLADES, FLORIDA

NATIONAL PARKS

I'VE VISITED:

HOPE TO VISIT:

THE MUSEUM OF BAD ART, MASSACHUSETTS

MUSEUMS AND GALLERIES

I'VE VISITED:

HOPE TO VISIT:

FALLINGWATER, PENNSYLVANIA, FRANK LLOYD WRIGHT

ARCHITECTURAL MASTERPIECES

I'VE VISITED:

HOPE TO VISIT:

PRENZLAUER BERG, BERLIN, GERMANY

NEIGHBORHOODS

I'VE WALKED:

HOPE TO WALK:

☐
☐
☐
☐
☐
☐
☐
☐
☐
☐
☐
☐
☐
☐
☐
☐
☐
☐
☐

ISTANBUL, TURKEY, WITH OUR GUIDE YAREN

CITY TOURS AND EXCURSIONS

I'VE DONE:

HOPE TO DO:

HARAJUKU, JAPAN

SHOPPING SPOTS, MARKETS, AND BAZAARS

I'VE SHOPPED:

HOPE TO SHOP:

CENTRAL PARK, NEW YORK CITY

CITY PARKS, GARDENS, AND PLAZAS

I'VE VISITED:

HOPE TO VISIT:

BLUE LAGOON, GRINDAVÍK, ICELAND

LAKES, LAGOONS, AND RIVERS

I'VE VISITED:

_____

_____

_____

_____

_____

_____

_____

_____

_____

_____

_____

_____

_____

_____

_____

_____

_____

_____

HOPE TO VISIT:

☐ _____

☐ _____

☐ _____

☐ _____

☐ _____

☐ _____

☐ _____

☐ _____

☐ _____

☐ _____

☐ _____

☐ _____

☐ _____

☐ _____

☐ _____

☐ _____

☐ _____

☐ _____

INGA'S MAGIC SHOW, RUSSIA

PERFORMING ARTS AND SPORTING EVENTS

I'VE SEEN:

HOPE TO SEE:

DIGGERLAND

AMUSEMENT PARKS

I'VE VISITED:

HOPE TO VISIT:

PÈRE LACHAISE, PARIS

CEMETERIES AND GRAVES

I'VE VISITED:

HOPE TO VISIT:

DHARAMSHALA, HIMACHAL PRADESH, INDIA

SPIRITUAL PLACES

I'VE VISITED:

_____

_____

_____

_____

_____

_____

_____

_____

_____

_____

_____

_____

_____

_____

_____

_____

_____

_____

_____

HOPE TO VISIT:

☐ _____

☐ _____

☐ _____

☐ _____

☐ _____

☐ _____

☐ _____

☐ _____

☐ _____

☐ _____

☐ _____

☐ _____

☐ _____

☐ _____

☐ _____

☐ _____

☐ _____

☐ _____

☐ _____

THE SKY

ROMANTIC PLACES

I'VE VISITED:

_____
_____
_____
_____
_____
_____
_____
_____
_____
_____
_____
_____
_____
_____
_____
_____
_____
_____

HOPE TO VISIT:

☐ _____
☐ _____
☐ _____
☐ _____
☐ _____
☐ _____
☐ _____
☐ _____
☐ _____
☐ _____
☐ _____
☐ _____
☐ _____
☐ _____
☐ _____
☐ _____
☐ _____
☐ _____

TOMATO FIGHT, COLOMBIA

FESTIVALS, PARADES, AND CARNIVALS

I'VE EXPERIENCED:

HOPE TO EXPERIENCE:

☐ ----------------------------

☐ ----------------------------

☐ ----------------------------

☐ ----------------------------

☐ ----------------------------

☐ ----------------------------

☐ ----------------------------

☐ ----------------------------

☐ ----------------------------

☐ ----------------------------

☐ ----------------------------

☐ ----------------------------

☐ ----------------------------

☐ ----------------------------

☐ ----------------------------

☐ ----------------------------

☐ ----------------------------

☐ ----------------------------

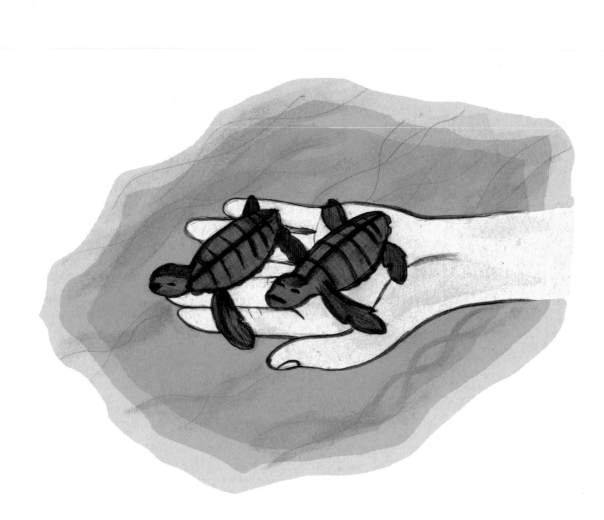

ENDANGERED SEA TURTLE COUNTING, TRINIDAD

VOLUNTEER TRAVEL

I'VE DONE:

HOPE TO DO:

BORA BORA

ISLANDS

I'VE VISITED:

_____

_____

_____

_____

_____

_____

_____

_____

_____

_____

_____

_____

_____

_____

_____

_____

_____

HOPE TO VISIT:

☐ _____

☐ _____

☐ _____

☐ _____

☐ _____

☐ _____

☐ _____

☐ _____

☐ _____

☐ _____

☐ _____

☐ _____

☐ _____

☐ _____

☐ _____

☐ _____

☐ _____

☐ _____

FLOYD'S PELICAN BAR, JAMAICA

BARS AND CLUBS

I'VE VISITED:

HOPE TO VISIT:

COOKING CLASS, THAILAND

EDUCATIONAL CLASSES AND CONFERENCES

I'VE TAKEN:

HOPE TO TAKE:

PIERRE DUBOIS, THE MIME

MEMORABLE PEOPLE AND GUIDES I'VE MET

www.SEATGUIDE.ORG

ABBA NESTING DOLLS

SOUVENIRS I'VE COME HOME WITH

MY NIECE

PEOPLE I SEND POSTCARDS TO

_____

_____

_____

_____

_____

_____

_____

_____

_____

_____

_____

_____

_____

_____

_____

_____

_____

_____

_____

TRAVELS WITH CHARLEY, STEINBECK

FAVORITE TRAVEL BOOKS

JIGSAW PUZZLES

IDEAS FOR A "STAYCATION"

MUD BATHS

LOCAL WEEKEND TRIP IDEAS

ROPES COURSE

SURPRISING THINGS I'VE DONE ON TRIPS

POOPING IN AN ALLEY

TRAVEL MISHAPS

ROAD TRIP 2010, FINDING A STRAY DOG

SERENDIPITOUS TRAVEL MOMENTS

SMALL ROOMS ON OUR CRUISE

TRAVEL DISAPPOINTMENTS

THE GO-GO'S "VACATION"

THE MOTORCYCLE DIARIES

MY FAVORITE TRAVEL FILMS AND TV SHOWS

THE STAIRS OF SELARÓN, RIO DE JANEIRO

UNIQUE LOCATIONS I'VE BEEN TO

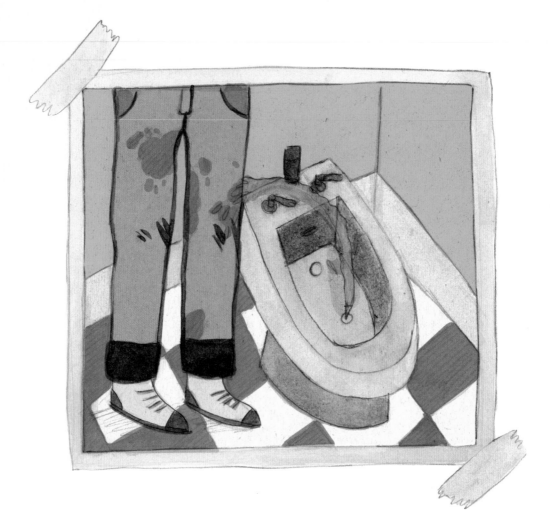

THE BIDET INCIDENT

MEMORABLE CULTURAL DIFFERENCES I'VE EXPERIENCED HERE AND ABROAD

SCOOT COUPES FOR TWO

MODES OF TRANSPORTATION I'VE TAKEN

1940, MAXWELL STREET, CHICAGO,
"BIRTHPLACE OF THE CHICAGO BLUES"

WHERE I'D TIME TRAVEL TO

DRINK MAI TAIS

THINGS I DO WHILE TRAVELING BUT NOT AT HOME

CHEESE FACTORY TOUR, HOLLAND

SILLY THINGS I'VE DONE ON TRIPS

PACK LIGHTER AND WASH CLOTHES ON THE ROAD

BEST TRAVEL TIPS

THE BERMUDA TRIANGLE

PLACES I HAVE LITTLE INTEREST IN VISITING

GINNY AND ED

PEOPLE I'VE TRAVELED WITH

THE ROOSEVELT HOTEL, HOLLYWOOD

PLACES I THOUGHT WERE HAUNTED OR CREEPY

LITTLE SAIGON, HOUSTON, TEXAS

EX-PAT COMMUNITIES I'VE VISITED

CHILDREN ARE THE SAME EVERYWHERE

THINGS I'VE LEARNED FROM TRAVELING

_____

_____

_____

_____

_____

_____

_____

_____

_____

_____

_____

_____

_____

_____

_____

_____

_____

_____

_____

BIG CITY DOG WALKERS

UNUSUAL THINGS I'VE WITNESSED

SAD: A SICK MONKEY

SAD AND HAPPY THINGS I'VE WITNESSED

SAD   HAPPY

FOOD! "THE GREEK PLATTER"

GETTING LOST

WHAT I LOVE AND HATE ABOUT TRAVELING

LOVE   HATE

WONDERLAND, WITH LEWIS CARROLL

PLACES I'VE TRAVELED VIA BOOKS, FILMS, AND TV

SEEING ELEPHANTS ON SAFARI IN KENYA

MOST MEMORABLE TRAVEL EXPERIENCES

INTERNATIONAL OUTLET ADAPTERS

MY TRAVEL AND PACKING CHECKLIST

- [ ] --
- [ ] --
- [ ] --
- [ ] --
- [ ] --
- [ ] --
- [ ] --
- [ ] --
- [ ] --
- [ ] --
- [ ] --
- [ ] --
- [ ] --
- [ ] --
- [ ] --
- [ ] --
- [ ] --
- [ ] --

FIRSTS

FIRST AIRPLANE RIDE

FIRST TRAIN RIDE

FIRST BOAT TRIP

FIRST ROAD TRIP

FIRST CAMPING TRIP

FIRST AMERICAN STATE

FIRST FOREIGN COUNTRY

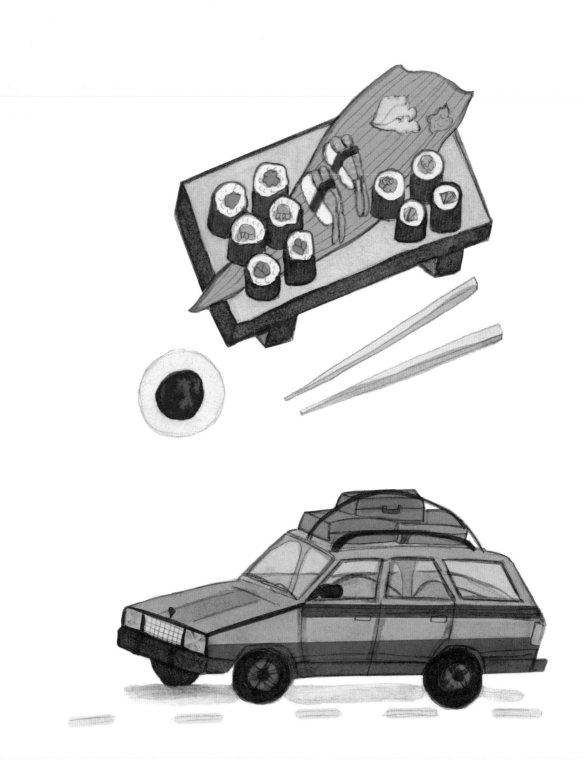

FIRST BEACH AND OCEAN

FIRST HOTEL

FIRST FRIEND ABROAD

FIRST FOREIGN FOOD

FIRST SOLITARY TRAVEL EXPERIENCE

FIRST TRAVEL COMPANION

FIRST FAMILY TRIP

FIRST GROUP TRAVEL

FIRST MOMENT OF AWE AND WONDER

FIRST UNLUCKY EXPERIENCE

FIRST LUCKY EXPERIENCE

FIRST TRAVEL INSPIRATION

FIRST

FIRST